The Story of Silk

To Ronnie Mae, Daniel, and Jonah, all together

Acknowledgments

I am indebted to Eric Booth and the Jim Thompson Thai Silk Company for guidance and important introductions to the silk weavers of northeastern Thailand. Their encouragement and private tour of the factory and farm at Pak Chong helped me a great deal in my understanding the science of silk weaving. I thank the silk growers and weavers of the villages of Huai Thaleng, Ban Kra Pho, Nong Hong, and Ban Tha Sawang for their warmth and hospitality. My guide and translator, Noppadon Tempsinpadung, was once again a great resource to me and my work. The concierge and staff of the Dusit Princess Hotel in Korat and the Shangri-La Hotel in Bangkok gave me shelter from the heat and encouraged this look into Thai culture. As I traveled, I purchased hundreds of yards of silk from the weavers that I met, photographed, and interviewed. Ting, Joy, and Lot of the fabulous Mazzaro dress-making shop in Bangkok saved the day by turning this cloth into perfectly tailored dresses for my wife, Ronnie Mae. Thanks to my agent and friend, Susie Cohen, and to my patient and insightful editor at Candlewick Press, Kate Fletcher, as well as to publisher Karen Lotz and designer Maryellen Hanley. As always, Daniel Sobol and Betty Bardige gave me insightful comments and suggestions to help me mold the story.

● ●

Sources

Cooper, Elizabeth K. *Silkworms and Science: The Story of Silk.* New York: Harcourt, Brace & World, 1961.
Drits, Diana. *Silkworm Moths.* Minneapolis: Lerner Publications, 2002.
Sharples, Jennifer. *Thai Silk.* Bangkok: Post Books, 1994.

Silkroad Foundation: http://www.silk-road.com

First edition 2012

Library of Congress Cataloging-in-Publication Data is available.

Library of Congress Catalog Card Number pending

ISBN 978-0-7636-4165-8

TLF 17 16 15 14 13 12
10 9 8 7 6 5 4 3 2 1

Printed in Dongguan, Guangdong, China

This book was typeset in Dante and Interstate.

Candlewick Press
99 Dover Street
Somerville, Massachusetts 02144

visit us at www.candlewick.com

THE STORY OF SILK

»From Worm Spit to Woven Scarves«

RICHARD SOBOL

CANDLEWICK PRESS

MYANMAR
(BURMA)

LAOS

• CHIANG MAI

THAILAND

Issan Province

NAKHON   HUA THA LENG
RATCHASIMA •   •   • BURI RAM

BANGKOK

CAMBODIA

VIETNAM

Andaman Sea

Gulf of
Thailand

MALAYSIA

• •

After my book The Life of Rice was published, I took copies back to Thailand
to share with the villagers I had written about. When I arrived, the farmers
had just completed the rice harvest and the dry season had begun. I asked the
farmers how they would spend the next few months until the rainy season began
and the rice growing process started up again. They answered with a single
word: "Worms." Worms? I asked if I had heard correctly. "Yes, worms!" the
farmers replied. "Millions and millions of worms!" Seeing the confused look on
my face, they laughed. One woman finally explained, "During the dry season,
we make silk — and to make silk, you need worms!" I instantly knew I had
the perfect subject for a new book — the story of silk!

Richard Sobol

Silk is the most magnificent of fabrics. It is shiny, strong, feels wonderful, and has been around for thousands of years. Though we might think of it as being worn only by kings and queens at royal parties or performers in lavish celebrations, in Thailand, farmers wear silk work clothes. Even though silk is precious and luxurious, it is also strong and useful.

No one is exactly sure how silk was first discovered. A popular legend traces the beginnings of silk to a Chinese empress named Chi Ling Zi, who lived about five thousand years ago. According to the story, Empress Chi loved nature and spent long hours each day roaming the palace gardens and climbing trees. One day, she discovered some cocoons in a mulberry tree and filled her pockets with them. Later, one of the cocoons slid out of her pocket and fell right into her cup of hot tea. When she tried to pull the cocoon out of her teacup, it started to unravel into one long piece of thread. She pulled and pulled and still did not reach the end. The thread was so long that she could hold one end of it and walk all the way from the garden to the courtyard, stretching the single strand far across the palace grounds. She immediately recognized that this material could be woven together to make a wonderful fabric. Together, Empress Chi and her husband, Emperor Huang Di, collected hundreds of cocoons from their mulberry trees and became the world's first silk farmers, or so the legend goes.

Though we don't know whether the tale of Empress Chi is true, we do know that since silk's discovery long ago, people have loved it. At first, silk was made exclusively in China. The Chinese held tightly to the secret of how it was produced for two thousand years. This made silk incredibly rare and extremely valuable. In ancient China, farmers used to pay taxes to the government with pieces of woven silk, trading it like money.

《 Thai women proudly show off a thirty-foot length of multicolored silk cloth that took them three weeks to create.

❯❯ Brightly colored unique Thai silk designs are offered for sale in shops in Issan Province.

From around 200 BCE through around 1400 CE, merchants and adventurers from Europe made long excursions across Asia on what became known as the Silk Road. These travelers journeyed to China in search of silk, hoping to purchase some of the precious fabric to bring back to sell in the West. In the late 1200s, the famous Italian explorer Marco Polo spent twenty-four years traveling fifteen thousand miles to China and back. When he returned, he published his adventures and discoveries in a book called *The Travels of Marco Polo*. He wrote about the many advances the Chinese people had made under the Yuan Dynasty: people bought and read paperbound books, ate rice from porcelain bowls, and wore silk clothes—even as pajamas! These were new and exciting concepts for most Europeans, and Marco Polo's story became very popular. By that time, some silkworm cocoons and the secret methods of silk production had been smuggled out of China, so other Asian and European countries were able to make their own silk.

Brightly colored unique Thai silk designs are offered for sale in shops in Issan Province.

Much of the silk produced around the world is woven on machines and has a consistently smooth feel to it. The silk produced in Thailand is woven entirely by hand and has a rougher, more free-form texture that reflects the craft of each artisan who works on it. Each piece

is unique to the village that created it. This individuality has added to Thai silk's reputation as some of the finest silk in the world.

« Small silk markets line the road near the silk-weaving villages of rural Thailand.

⋙ Bicycles share the road as children get rides home from school in the late afternoon.

After leaving my home in Massachusetts and flying for twenty-two hours, I arrive in Bangkok, the capital of Thailand, tired but excited—ready to learn how Thai silk is made. I stop by my favorite noodle shop for an early breakfast before meeting up with my friend and translator, Noppadon. Don, as he's called, was my guide on my earlier trip to Thailand, so we are good friends now.

I jump into Don's car, and we head straight toward the remote villages in the countryside where silk is made. To avoid the crazy morning traffic jams, we leave the city before sunrise. The journey to Issan Province takes more than six hours—first on the highway and then on a country road that branches off near the village of Huai Thalaeng (whay tah-leng). Along the way, I watch other vehicles passing by—mostly the small two-wheeled vehicles that are common in Thailand, with only a few other cars and pickup trucks on the road. It never ceases to amaze me how many people can squeeze onto a bicycle!

After bouncing for an hour on a bumpy side road, we pass a forty-foot-long statue of a silkworm—a unique sight, indeed! Don stops the car so I can take a photo of this odd-looking worm. I ask Don if silkworms are like the earthworms we have back home in the United States, and he tells me that silkworms are not even actually worms! Since silkworms are the larvae, or immature form, of moths, they are technically caterpillars. Although everyone calls them silkworms—even scientists, who gave them the scientific name *Bombyx mori,* which means "silkworm of the mulberry tree"—the creatures that make silk are not worms at all.

I photograph the giant sculpture, then Don and I sit on the smiling cement statue while he tells me more about the non-worm worms.

"Silkworms are delicate creatures," he explains. "Just like any pet, they need to be cared for and fed every day in order to survive in captivity, where they are completely dependent on people to keep them alive. If the farmers do not feed them a steady supply of mulberry leaves, they die.

"Silkworms are also very picky eaters. The leaves of the mulberry tree are the only things in the whole world that they will eat. From the time the tiny eggs hatch, silkworms spend the first twenty-eight days of their lives doing nothing but eating mulberry leaves.

"Look over there," he says, pointing to a large green plot that borders a rice field. "Those farmers are growing mulberry trees to make sure they have plenty of juicy leaves for the silkworms to eat."

When Don and I finally arrive at the village of Huai Thalaeng several hours later, the dirt-packed roads seem much quieter than I remembered from my last visit. Walking slowly through the town, I see tall stacks of flat woven-grass baskets, each covered tightly with a bright cotton cloth. I also notice looms with small wooden benches and long bamboo poles suspended off the ground underneath them. Many of the looms have carved wooden spools and partially completed weavings stretched across them. The looms mystify me: I see hundreds of strands of silk threads crisscrossing back and forth, but I have no idea how a weaver would even begin to get all those threads to make a piece of fabric.

Though I see evidence of silk making all around me, I don't see any people! Listening closely, the only sounds I hear are the *cluck-cluck*s of the chickens strutting in the yard of one of the houses nearby. I wander

⌃ Mulberry leaves are harvested throughout the day so there will be fresh leaves for the hungry worms.

>> A villager fixes a flat tire while some free-roaming chickens look on.

⌄ Thai boys meditate at the temple during their school vacation to learn the basic teachings of Buddhism.

around the village until I hear a faint but steady *woosh, woosh, woosh* sound. *That must be the sound of a spinning wheel turning,* I think.

I walk toward the sound and emerge into a small courtyard, where at last I discover that there is at least one other person here in the village with us! A man is sitting in the courtyard spinning a wheel, but it is not the wheel of a silk loom, rather the flat tire of a bicycle wheel being fixed. I ask the bike mechanic where everybody else has gone.

"Today is the start of the school holiday, so the boys are at the temple studying with the monks," he says. He goes on to explain that all boys in Thailand are expected to learn the first ten lessons of becoming a holy Buddhist monk.

"The monks are our most respected teachers," he explains. "A monk learns all two hundred and twenty-seven lessons, but our boys just get a beginners' lesson during their break from school. While they are studying, their parents and sisters usually bring them lunch, so that is why it's so quiet here now."

"But what about the silkworms?" I ask,

remembering what I've learned about how carefully they must be tended to. "Doesn't someone have to be here to look after them?"

"You're right," he says with a laugh. "The worms need lunch, too, but they all got fed a big pile of leaves just before everyone left—and the rest of the children should be back to feed them again soon."

Shortly after he says this, a group of girls comes running down the street carrying a jump rope that seems as long as Empress Chi's silk thread. One of them spots me and waves.

"Mr. Richard is back!" I hear her tell her friends. The girls turn and whisper to one another, then erupt into laughter.

"Hey, look—it's the camera man!" she hollers. "Are we going to be in another book?"

I smile and reply, "Perhaps! I am working on another book, but this one is all about silk."

"Oooh! We can show you our silk dresses!" one says.

Another shouts, "We will be the super-models of silk!" and they all start giggling at once.

"Well," I reply, "it's been a long time since I did any fashion photography, but for the best silk models in Thailand, I'll do it!"

The girls make me promise to take photographs of them in their finest silk dresses before I leave, and then they shriek with joy and run off to finish their chores.

⌃ Individual strands of natural silk fiber are wound together to make a thick roll of silk thread.

The women of the village have also returned from the temple, and all of a sudden, the silk-making process begins again. One by one, the looms begin to shuffle up and down, long reels of silk unwind, wheels start to spin, and kettles of hot water come to a boil on open charcoal fires. All the stages of creating silk are happening at the same time! Everywhere I look, I see something interesting happening, and I hardly know where to point my camera. My confusion must be apparent, because a woman beside me says, "Don't worry, Richard. We will explain it all to you. I promise that before you leave here you will be an expert on Thai silk!"

I'm surprised that this woman knows my name, but then she introduces herself as Mrs. Sanachong and says, "I understand if you don't recognize me. The last time you saw me, I was dressed in layers of clothing and farming rice, not making silk!"

My face lights up as I remember who she is, "Yes!" I reply as we both break into smiles.

"Sit down," she says. "And let me tell you all about silkworms." I set my heavy camera gear on the ground and sit down on the worn teak bench next to her.

"When the dry season begins, the mulberry trees start to blossom. At this time, we get a delivery of teeny-tiny silkworm eggs that come from a giant farm near Bangkok. Forty thousand eggs come together on one sheet of letter paper. When we get them, they look like tiny black dots no bigger than poppy seeds. As long as they are covered, the eggs will rest, but as soon as they are uncovered, they wake up and start to hatch."

Mrs. Sanachong shows me a large basket and pulls back the cloth covering. I peek inside and see hundreds of white striped silkworms scattered on a bed of green leaves.

As I watch the worms wiggle and squirm, Mrs. Sanachong taps me on the shoulder. "I know you will want to take lots of pictures of them, but we can't leave them uncovered for long in this dry hot

⌄ Hundreds of silkworms live together in a basket, where they munch on fresh mulberry leaves day and night.

air or they will overheat and die." I quickly take a few photos, and then Mrs. Sanachong covers the worms back up.

"You can see that silkworms have a three-inch-long marshmallowy body with a lot of little legs. They also have a tiny point of a mouth at one end with two strong jaws that cut into mulberry leaves like scissors. They slice, then dice, and chew, chew, chew. The worms are always eating!"

She shows me one of the leaves from the worms' basket. "See how they eat around the edge of the soft leaves, making a tighter circle towards the center?" The way the silkworms eat leaves reminds me of a lawn mower going around and around as it cuts through a yard full of overgrown grass.

"With all this eating," Mrs. Sanachong continues, "the worms are constantly growing. But while their bodies expand, their skin stays the same size. So then they must wiggle out from that tight casing in a process called molting. As soon as the worm molts, a new layer of skin immediately begins growing around it. They will do this three more times as they grow, each time exchanging a tight layer of skin for a new larger size. During this period of steady growth and constant feeding, each tiny silkworm will eat fifty times its body weight," she says. "That would be like you or me eating a car or bus. We would explode!"

As I think about how much work—and food—it takes to keep the silkworms happy, I hear the girls that I spoke with earlier. They are more serious now, talking softly and sitting down at a table nearby. There is a stack of baskets beside them.

Silkworms are picky eaters and will eat only the freshest of leaves. Any that are wilted or damaged are discarded.

↑ Thai girls on poop patrol clean each cocoon by hand.

"Are they feeding the worms again?" I ask, motioning toward the girls.

"No," Mrs. Sanachong says, smiling. "They are on poop patrol!"

"I've got to see this," I say, and we walk over so I can get a better look. Mrs. Sanachong continues her explanation: "All that eating makes for a lot of worm poop, so the trays need to be cleaned all the time to stay fresh."

"We have to pull the poop off *every* cocoon," one of the girls tells me.

"We get this job because our fingers are small and fast," says another, speaking to me while keeping her eyes glued to the mountain of yellow puffs in front of her. "Before the thread can be cooked and unwound, it must be completely clean and perfectly yellow—poopless!" she says as they all break into giggles.

I watch each cocoon pass through cleaning and inspection as the girls hand them around. As soon as they finish with the hundreds of yellow puffs in one basket, another basket is waiting right behind it. The task looks endless. There are so many cocoons!

When one basket is full of smooth, clean, poop-free cocoons, a

woman comes to take it away. Mrs. Sanachong motions for me to fol-
low her toward a smoldering cauldron. I watch closely as the woman
places the basket down in front of her, next to the blackened iron pot.

She picks up a few of the yellow cocoons in her hand and rolls them
between her fingers. She explains to me that after a month of nonstop
eating, the silkworm has had enough food and is now a fully grown pupa, with two tiny pipes called glands that run from head to tail on its bottom side. Each gland has a different juice in it. When the two juices get mixed together, they become strong, like epoxy glue. The silkworm spits out tiny droplets of these liquids, one from each gland, and when they touch, they stick together. As more and more spit is released, it slowly joins together to make a single strand of silk!

For three days, the silkworm steadily produces these two liquids while rolling over and over, creating one long unbroken silk thread. At first, the yellow threads look like a light airy cotton ball, but as more and more layers are added, they become a

⌄ It takes thousands of cocoons to make just one dress out of Thai silk.

round yellow cocoon surrounding the worm. That is a big job for a little worm, and once the cocoon is thick enough, the worm goes to sleep, or hibernates. If the worm is left undisturbed, it will sleep for up to two weeks and then wake up as a moth, with new wings ready to flap and fly.

"But where are all the moths, then?" I ask, looking around for the "moth station." "And how does a yellow cocoon like that turn into a multicolored skirt or a scarf?"

The woman checks the cauldron and sees that the water is simmering.

"Let me show you," she says, and points into the steaming pot. I watch as she slowly pours the cocoons into the bubbling liquid.

The slow cooking gently releases the threads into single strands. The yellow of the thread is so bright! She uses a long bamboo fork to help loosen the strands as they float to the surface. As I watch, I learn that in order to unwind the silk thread from the cocoons, the life cycle of the worm must end.

⩔ Cocoons cook slowly in a heavy iron kettle, releasing fine yellow threads which are gathered in a wheel above the kettle.

"These silkworms won't turn into moths," she explains. "But their cocoons will create silk thread and the worms themselves will make a tasty snack, so at least no part of the worms are wasted!"

The shiny thread is removed from the pot by attaching it to a spinning wheel, where it emerges from the dark cauldron and starts to dry in the hot tropical air. Loops of thread wrap around the hoops as they are slowly turned by hand. Some of these spinning wheels are made of wood, and others are rigged from bent bicycle rims. As I watch the spinning wheel drag the thread out of the pot, I begin to believe the legend of Empress Chi: I see now that one thread of silk seems to go on forever!

Once all the thread has been removed from the pot, the boiled worms are skimmed off the top and

≪ Many silk threads are spun together to make a stronger one for sewing and weaving.

≫ Boiled silkworms make a gourmet meal for some — but not for me!

spooned into bowls for a group of men who have just sat down at a table for dinner. They invite me to join them, but although I love seeing, photographing, and even touching the worms, I do not want to eat them!

"You are really missing out," the men exclaim, "but hey, that means more for us!" Laughing, they dip the boiled silkworms into red-pepper sauce and pop them into their mouths.

That night, I realize that while I've learned more than I ever thought there was to know

∧ Different-colored threads are woven together on a loom to make patterns and designs.

about silkworms, there is still one very important part of making silk that I do not understand at all. I am a clever mechanic and love all sorts of gadgets, but I remain completely baffled when I look at a loom. What keeps all those threads together? How *do* they do it?

The next day, I ask if I can join in while a popular local woman known as Auntie gives the girls a weaving lesson. They will be working on the looms and practicing hand-tying patterns in a special Thai style known

≪ Silk thread is hand tied in a traditional Thai style know as *matmee.*

≫ Natural silk is dipped into a boiling pot of magenta dye. This intense color is enhanced with synthetic pigments.

as *matmee. Matmee* uses silk thread that has been tie-dyed into bold colors and allows a weaver to make multicolored patterns in her design. Before the thread is woven, the long spools are dipped into boiling vats of colored dye, often using pigments that are harvested locally from native roots, tree bark, or herbs. Auntie is a master at getting the dye the exact color she wants and is well known for her prized silk creations.

When I arrive, there are already a few women busy pulling and pushing the wooden poles of their looms in the courtyard. The girls

are squeezed together on the bench in the center, and I join them with all my photography equipment to capture the lesson.

First, Auntie leans over and picks up a thread. "See how these threads go up and down? Those are called the warp," she says, and the girls all nod. "The warp threads stay tight and move up and down as the cross threads, known as the weft, are passed through and woven over them using this wooden stick called a shuttle. The ends of the shuttle are carved smooth and pointed at each end so they can slide easily over the warp threads."

《 A shuttle carries teal weft thread through the warp threads of the loom.

⌃ Foot pedals move the threads up and down as warp and weft threads are woven together.

As she talks, she pulls pieces of the loom with both her hands and her feet. It would be hard enough for me to operate the loom with my hands, let alone with my hands *and* feet! But Auntie is a masterful weaver, so she continues to explain as she weaves.

"You can see that since my feet control the levers that pull the warp threads up and down, I can use my hands to move the shuttle from one side to the other."

The girls nod again and say, "Sure, Auntie" and "That looks easy." As they take turns trying it out, I think how lucky I am that I am just here to take photographs, as I would surely fail at actually weaving! I look at the maze of thread and start to see how it is slowly being woven into fabric.

Although the people of this village weave most of their silk into clothing for themselves, a few special pieces will be set aside to sell. Silk fabric will never rot or fade and can be saved for months or even years. Since it is easy to store, families

≫ Some silk from the village is sold to buyers who sell it in dress shops in Bangkok and around the world.

can sell a few pieces of silk when they have used up their cash from the rice crop.

In Issan, everybody wears silk. Women wear silk blouses, dresses, and long skirts; men wear tailored dress shirts and wraparound leggings called *lon chee;* and even the kids have silk clothes for special occasions. Which reminds me: now that the weaving lesson is over, it is finally time for my friends, the young silk supermodels, to show off their special dresses!

As the girls parade down the street in their silk clothes and then sit together on the steps of a house, one of their older sisters stands with me to narrate this unique runway show.

"Each of these young women knows every part of the long process of silk making," she says. "Someone in our village touched every inch of the fabric and pulled every line of thread to make these dresses from them. And they helped to feed the worms and then cleaned the poop from their cocoons, so, these dresses are very special to them!"

I see how proud the girls are of the silk that their village has made and take some photographs while they model.

⌄ Thai girls proudly model their silk dresses, completely handmade in their own village.

⌃ Silk from Thai villages is famous and well known for its high quality and unique designs.

"And one more thing," one of the girls says, handing me a silk scarf. "This is some of our silk. We want you to have this so you will always remember our village!"

I thank her from the bottom of my heart, and then, as I put down my camera, I look closely at the lovely piece of silk in my hand. Running my fingers over the smooth fabric, I recall everything that went into making it, all of which happened right here in this small village. I think of how many hands went into creating this one piece of cloth. I remember the legend of the Chinese empress and her teacup five thousand years ago. Although no one knows if that story is completely true or not, I like to think there is some truth to it. It would surely take a miracle, like a cocoon accidentally dropping into hot tea, to discover that a beautiful scarf like this could come from a long string of worm spit.

⌃ Fluffy cocoons are picked from branches by hand once the worms are hibernating.

Silk Facts

The production of silk and raising worms is called sericulture.

The silkworm is not really a worm. It is the caterpillar, or larva, of a silkmoth whose Latin name, *Bombyx mori,* means "silkworm of the mulberry tree."

Silkworms eat only the leaves from mulberry trees.

As it grows, a silkworm will shed its skin and molt four times.

To make one pound of silk, 1,500 silkworms must consume 100 pounds of mulberry leaves.

When fully grown, a silkworm weighs 10,000 times more than it did at birth.

When it is about thirty to thirty-five days old, a silkworm starts to spin a cocoon, which will take three to four days to complete.

It takes about 110 cocoons to make enough silk for a necktie, 630 for a blouse, and almost 5,000 to make enough silk for one long dress.

It takes forty hours of spinning by hand to make one pound of Thai silk thread.

The thread of one cocoon is a single strand almost one mile in length.

Silk is made up of protein, much like human hair or sheep's wool.

Silk is one of the strongest natural fibers. Some of the earliest airplanes had silk stretched over their wings since it gave good strength for its weight.

≫ Flat round baskets hold hundreds of freshly spun cocoons.

Silk is a naturally adjusting fiber. It is cool to wear in the summer and warm in the winter.

China is the leading producer of silk. Thailand is the fifth.

The United States is the largest buyer of silk in the world.

« Dyed silk threads are hung up to dry.

⌄ It takes one week of hand weaving to make just three feet of silk cloth.

Glossary

cocoon a protective case spun by the larva of moths

gland a body part or group of cells that produces and secretes a liquid

hibernation a dormant state resembling sleep

larva the immature form of an insect

loom a machine for weaving thread into cloth

matmee a Thai silk weaving pattern involving many colors

molt to shed an outer covering, which is then replaced by new growth

pupa the stage of life when an insect weaves a cocoon and hibernates

shuttle carries the weft thread as it weaves through the warp

warp a set of threads running lengthwise in a loom

weft a set of threads running across a loom, which interlace with the warp threads